Sugarpaste
CAKE DECORATING
WITH STEP-BY-STEP INSTRUCTIONS

MARY FORD

ACKNOWLEDGEMENTS

MARY FORD ACKNOWLEDGES WITH THANKS THE
ASSISTANCE GIVEN IN THE PREPARATION OF
THIS BOOK BY

STAN AND BETTY ODDY

and

RAY HOVELL

(THE TUTORIAL MANAGER OF HER SCHOOL OF CAKE ARTISTRY)

PUBLISHED BY MARY FORD CAKE ARTISTRY CENTRE LTD.
28-30 SOUTHBOURNE GROVE, SOUTHBOURNE, BOURNEMOUTH, DORSET, ENGLAND BH6 3RA
ALL RIGHTS RESERVED. NO PART OF THIS PUBLICATION MAY BE REPRODUCED, STORED IN A
RETRIEVAL SYSTEM, OR TRANSMITTED, IN ANY FORM OR BY ANY MEANS, ELECTRONIC,
MECHANICAL, PHOTOCOPYING, RECORDING OR OTHERWISE, WITHOUT THE PERMISSION OF
MARY FORD CAKE ARTISTRY CENTRE LTD.

PRINTED AND BOUND IN GREAT BRITAIN BY PURNELL BOOK PRODUCTION LTD.

ISBN 0946429 10 3

MARY FORD STRESSES THE IMPORTANCE OF ALL ASPECTS OF CAKE ARTISTRY, BUT ALWAYS GIVE SPECIAL EMPHASIS TO THE
BASIC INGREDIENTS AND UNRESERVEDLY RECOMMEND THE USE OF 'TATE & LYLE' ICING SUGAR.

CONTENTS

THE AUTHOR

The name Mary Ford is inextricably linked with Cake Decoration and Mary Ford is acknowledged by the Craft as a world leader in cake design and artistry.

Mary and her husband Michael have run the very successful Mary Ford Cake Artistry Centre in Bournemouth, England for the last 15 years. Working with the school Mary developed her unique artistic and teaching talent which she was encouraged in 1981 to make available to a wider audience through books. Mary's first book "101 Cake Designs" was an immediate best seller and it has since been followed by a whole series of successful titles.

Using the step-by-step approach with detailed photographs (taken by Michael) the most complicated and daunting cakes have been simplified. Editorial instructions appear with each photograph to guide the decorator.

Much of Mary's time is now concentrated on preparing a great variety of cake (and other) designs for her books. However, she remains involved in answering cake decoration queries from around the world and passing on her own knowledge and standards to amateurs and professionals. Mary is also active in designing her unique range of Mary Ford Cake Artistry equipment.

INTRODUCTION

This new book by Mary Ford combines royal icing artistry with fruit or sponge cakes covered in sugarpaste. It is set out with the traditional Mary Ford step-by-step photographs with accompanying instruction and editorial.

The book is divided into Three parts:

Part One includes all the basic information. Recipes for cakes, fillings, coverings, pastes and royal icing are fully documented. Instruction is given, with photographs, of the making and colouring of both sugarpaste and flowerpaste.

Part Two includes detailed description and photographs on how to make a wide variety of sugar flowers. The flowers include carnations, freesias, sweet peas, daffodils and roses. Instruction is given on how to assemble the flowers to make a spray or a small bouquet for the top or side of a cake.

Part Three includes some lovely wedding and celebration cakes decorated with delicate sprays of flowers or Christmas roses, all finished off with piping, edgings and inscriptions in royal icing. Cakes in this section include the dancing girl, Zoe; a wise owl, Kerry; a lovely bouncing puppy, Treacle; and Violetta, the wedding cake decorated with crystallised edible violets.

Mary's creative talent is once again on display in this book. The quality of photographs is sufficiently detailed to give the decorator the opportunity to see and understand each stage of the process, even in some of the intricate floral designs of Part Two. Assistance is also given by the inclusion of template drawings, ribbon insertion instructions, piping and crimping techniques.

CAKE AND FLOWER
PICTORIAL INDEX

6

CARNATION
PAGE 36

RHIAN
PAGE 54

TRIXIE
PAGE 82

CHRISTMAS ROSE
PAGE 66

NIKKI
PAGE 76

SECRET LOVE
PAGE 47

CHRYSTAL
PAGE 50

SNOWBAND
PAGE 69

VERINA
PAGE 78

SWEET
PEA
PAGE 34

ANNAMARIE
PAGE 70

CHERILYN
PAGE 90

VIOLETTA
PAGE 84

DEIRDRIE
PAGE 58

ROSE
PAGE 28

LILY
PAGE 40

BEATRICE
PAGE 17

DAFFODIL
PAGE 30

HARMONY
PAGE 88

7

FRUIT CAKE

INGREDIENTS FOR A 5″ ROUND CAKE

INGREDIENTS

2 ozs/57 g/½ cup PLAIN FLOUR
2ozs/57g/⅓ cup BROWN SUGAR
2 ozs/57 g/¼ cup BUTTER
2½ ozs/71 g/½ cup CURRANTS
2½ ozs/71 g/½ cup SULTANAS
1 oz/28 g/3 tblspns SEEDLESS RAISINS
1 oz/28 g/3 tblspns GLACÉ CHERRIES
1½ ozs/42 g/4½ tblspns MIXED PEEL
¾ oz/21 g/2½ tblspns GROUND ALMONDS
½ fl oz/2 tspn BRANDY OR RUM
1 LARGE FRESH EGG
1 pinch NUTMEG
1 pinch MIXED SPICE
1 pinch SALT
¼ LEMON ZEST & JUICE

PREPARATION First line your tin with a double layer of buttered greaseproof paper. Then clean and prepare the fruit, halve the cherries. Mix all fruit together with lemon zest. Sift flour, spices and salt.

METHOD Beat the butter until light. Add sugar to butter and beat again until light. Gradually add egg, beating in thoroughly after each addition. Stir in ground almonds. Fold in flour and spices. Finally, add fruit together with brandy or rum and lemon juice. Mix well together and transfer to tin.

It is most important to follow the exact measurements and mixture of the foregoing ingredients.

In baking the cake initially, if one pint of water is placed in a meat tray in the bottom of the oven, this will create sufficient humidity to keep the top of the cake moist and ensure level results in baking. Remove water after half baking time.

When the cake is baked, leave it in the tin (pan) for one day, remove from tin (pan) then brush the appropriate quantity of soaking mixture on the cake. Wrap cake in waxed paper and leave in a cupboard for three weeks. When the waxed paper becomes sticky, this means that moisture is seeping out, a sure sign that the cake is mature. If more liquid is required, add just before marzipanning. A cake needs no more than three weeks to mature.

Bake at 275°F, 140°C, Gas Mark 1

LARGER CAKE INGREDIENTS

If a larger cake is required, use the following table to obtain the correct quantity of ingredients.

FOR EXAMPLE –
(1) *If a 9″ heart-shaped cake is required* look down the 'Cake Tin Size' column to – 9 –. Follow along that line until the 'Heart' column is reached. the figure – 5 – means that the above ingredients must be multiplied FIVE TIMES to make a 9″ heart-shaped cake.
(2) *For an 11″ square cake,* The ingredients need to be multiplied SEVEN TIMES.

TIN SIZE	ROUND	SQ	HEART	HEX	BAKING TIME IN HOURS
5″	1	1½	1½	1	1½–1¾
6″	1½	2	2	1½	1¾–2
7″	2	3	3	2	2½–3
8″	3	4	4	3	3½–4
9″	4	5	5	4	4–4½
10″	5	6	6	5	4¼–4¾
11″	6	7	7	6	4½–5
12″	7	8	8	7	5–5½

SOAKING MIXTURE

Equal quantities of Rum, Sherry and Glycerine or spirits of choice. 1 tbls. per 1 lb of cake when required.

CONVERSION TABLES

WEIGHT		SIZE	
IMPERIAL	METRIC	IMPERIAL	METRIC
½ oz	14 g	5 ins	12.5 cm
1 oz	28 g	6 ins	15 cm
2 oz	57 g	7 ins	18 cm
3 oz	85 g	8 ins	20.5 cm
4 oz	113 g	9 ins	23 cm
5 oz	142 g	10 ins	25.5 cm
6 oz	170 g	11 ins	28 cm
7 oz	198 g	12 ins	30.5 cm
8 oz	227 g	13 ins	33 cm
9 oz	255 g	14 ins	35.5 cm
10 oz	284 g	15 ins	38 cm
11 oz	312 g	16 ins	40.5 cm
12 oz	340 g		
13 oz	369 g		
14 oz	397 g		
15 oz	425 g		
16 oz	454 g		

RECIPES

HEAVY GENOESE SPONGE CAKE RECIPE

INGREDIENTS

3 oz/85 g/6 tblspns BUTTER
3 oz/85 g/6 tblspns MARGARINE
6 oz/170 g/¾ cup CASTER SUGAR
3 EGGS, lightly beaten
6 oz/170 g/1½ cups SELF-RAISING FLOUR SIEVED

PREPARATION. First line your tin (pans) with greased greaseproof paper.

METHOD. Cream butter and margarine. Add sugar and beat until light in colour and fluffy in texture. Add the egg a little at a time beating after each addition. Carefully fold in the flour.
Bake: 190°C, 375°F, Gas 5. 20-25 minutes.

½ recipe makes 1 @ 8″ Rd sponge
or 1 @ 7″ Sq
1 recipe makes 1 @ 10″ Rd sponge
or 1 @ 9″ Sq
1½ recipe makes 1 @ 12″ Rd sponge
or 1 @ 11″ Sq

BUTTERCREAM

INGREDIENTS

6 ozs/170 g/¾ cup BUTTER
12 ozs/340 g/2⅔ cups ICING SUGAR SIEVED
1 oz/28 g/3 tblspns WARM WATER

METHOD. Beat the butter until light. Then beat in the icing sugar a little at a time. Add and beat in the water until the mixture is light and fluffy. Add colour and flavour, if required.

GUM ARABIC SOLUTION

Boil 3 ozs of water. Remove from heat and immediately whisk in 1 oz of gum arabic powder. Leave to cool. Remove any surface film and store in a refrigerator until required.

ROYAL ICING RECIPE

INGREDIENTS

½ oz/14 g/1½ tblspns POWDERED EGG WHITE
3 fl oz/3 tblspns/⅜ cup COLD WATER
1 lb/454 kg/3½ cups ICING SUGAR, SIEVED

OR

3 EGG WHITES (separated the day before)
1 lb/454 g/3½ cups ICING SUGAR

PREPARATION. All equipment used must be perfectly cleaned and sterilised. Pour water into a jug and stir in powdered egg white. This will go lumpy and necessitates standing the mixture for one hour, stirring occasionally. Then strain through a muslin.

METHOD. Pour solution or egg whites into a mixing bowl and place the icing sugar on top. A drop of blue colour (color) may be added for white icing. Beat on slow speed for approximately 15-20 minutes or until the right consistency is obtained. (If powdered egg white is used the Royal Icing will keep in good condition for 2 weeks. Fresh egg whites will deteriorate quicker). Store Royal Icing in sealed container in a cool place.

GLYCERINE
TABLE FOR USE

For soft-cutting icing (per 1 lb or 454 g or 3½ cups of ready-made Royal Icing) use 1 teaspoon of glycerine for the bottom tier of a 3-tier wedding cake.
2 teaspoons of glycerine for the middle tier.
3 teaspoons of glycerine for the top tier, or for single tier cakes.
(N.B. Glycerine only to be added after Royal Icing has been made.)
NO GLYCERINE IN ROYAL ICING FOR RUNOUTS OR No. 1 WORK.

SUGARPASTE

Sugarpaste is a firm, sweet paste which is generally rolled out into sheet form (in a similar manner to marzipan/almond paste) to cover cakes. It can be coloured and flavoured to suit personal choice.

INGREDIENTS

1 lb/454 g/4 cups ICING SUGAR
4 level teaspoons POWDERED GELATINE
2 teaspoons LIQUID GLUCOSE
4 tablespoons WATER

1. Sieve all the icing sugar into a bowl.

3. Gently heat the saucepan until the gelatine dissolves (occasionally stirring with a wooden spoon). Add the glucose to the mixture and remove saucepan from the heat.

2. Pour all the water into a stainless steel or non-stick saucepan. Then sprinkle the powdered gelatine on to the water.

4. Add a quarter of the icing sugar to the mixture and stir.

5. Keep adding icing sugar, which should be stirred with the spoon (to ensure lumps don't form). When the mixture is too stiff to stir, remove the wooden spoon.

8. Now knead the mixture with the palm of the hand until a clean, clear texture is obtained. This is now sugarpaste.

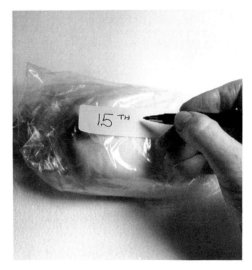

6. Continue adding icing sugar, which must now be mixed by hand.

9. Place the sugarpaste into a polythene bag and label it with the date it was made (as it should be used within two weeks). Leave to mature for 24 hours.

7. When the mixture becomes a thick paste, remove it from the saucepan and place on a smooth surface. Add the remaining icing sugar by kneading the paste between fingers and thumbs.

FLAVOURING AND COLOURING
SUGARPASTE

1. Ensure there is sufficient sugarpaste to complete the whole project (as it is difficult to match the colours at a later date).

2. Knead the sugarpaste into a ball and remove any crust particles. Now add flavouring of choice (e.g. kirsch, orange, lemon, rosewater) and again knead the mixture.

3. Dip a cocktail stick into colour of choice (liquid or paste) and wipe on to the sugarpaste. BE PATIENT and add a little colour at a time so that overcolouring is avoided.

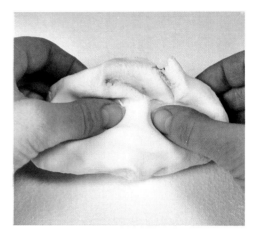

4. Thoroughly mix in the colour by repeatedly tearing and mixing the sugarpaste between fingers and thumbs.

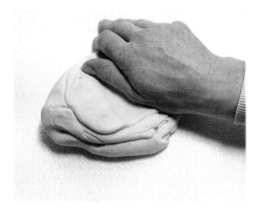

5. To remove any puffiness, knead the sugarpaste with the palm of the hand on a clean flat surface.

6. To test colour correctness and eveness, roll out the sugarpaste on a flat surface. If more colour is required, repeat No's 3, 4 and 5 and test again. if colour is spread unevenly, repeat No's 4 and 5 and test again.

FLOWER PASTE

Flower paste is a firm, sweet paste which is generally used for modelling hand-made cake artistry flowers.

INGREDIENTS
2 ozs/57 g/½ cup CORNFLOUR
14 ozs/400 g/3½ cups ICING SUGAR (SIEVED)
¾ oz/21 g/2½ tblspn GUM TRAGACANTH
¾ oz/21 g/2½ tblspn GLUCOSE
1 oz/28 g/3 tblspn COLD WATER
¾ oz/21 g/2½ tblspn WHITE FAT

1. Weigh all ingredients carefully and place the icing sugar, cornflour and gum tragacanth on greaseproof paper.

4. Thoroughly mix the ingredients (on a 'slow' machine or by hand with a wooden spoon).

2. Tip the dry ingredients through a sieve into a bowl. Repeat twice more.

5. The paste is properly mixed when 'clear' – does not stick to the side of the bowl.

3. Add remaining ingredients into the bowl.

6. Mould the paste into a ball, place into a polythene bag and leave to mature for at least 24 hours.

PREPARING A GENOESE SPONGE BEFORE COVERING WITH
SUGARPASTE

1. Make and bake two round genoese sponges to the size required. Cool sponges in a refrigerator for one hour (to enable easier handling).

2. Immediately after removing them from the refrigerator, trim off top and side crusts from the sponges.

3. Picture showing a sponge with the crusts removed. (Note: it is very important to obtain even and flat surfaces at this stage).

4. Spread flavoured and coloured buttercream of choice over the top of one sponge. Place on a cake board.

5. Place second sponge on top and thinly spread buttercream over the top surface.

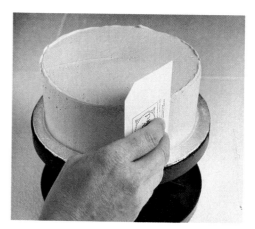

6. Thinly spread buttercream around the sponge-side. Return the coated sponge to the refrigerator for at least one hour before coating with sugarpaste.

COVERING A PREPARED GENOESE SPONGE WITH
SUGARPASTE

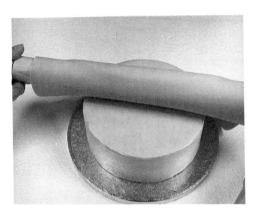

1. Roll out a sheet of coloured and flavoured sugarpaste of sufficient size to cover the top and side of the sponge (using icing sugar for dusting).

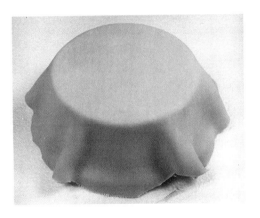

2. Cover the sponge with the sheet of sugarpaste (using a rolling pin to transfer the sugarpaste).

3. Rotating a flat hand on the sponge-top, smooth the sugarpaste (and, thus, expel the trapped air). Then gently smooth the sugarpaste to the shape of the sponge-side.

4. Trim surplus sugarpaste from the sponge-base, using a sharp, clean knife.

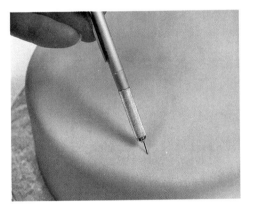

5. Remove any remaining pockets of air (which are trapped between the sugarpaste and buttercream) by puncturing them with a stainless steel needle.

6. Smooth entire sugarpaste surface with a cake smoother. Leave to dry for 24 hours before decorating.

HOW TO MARZIPAN A SQUARE FRUIT CAKE BEFORE COVERING WITH
SUGARPASTE

1. Place the fruit cake on a suitable cake-board (with top of cake uppermost).

2. Fill-in cake imperfections with marzipan and then brush boiling apricot puree over the top and sides.

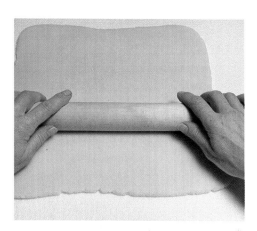

3. Roll out a ¼″ thick sheet of marzipan of sufficient size to amply cover the whole cake (using icing sugar for dusting).

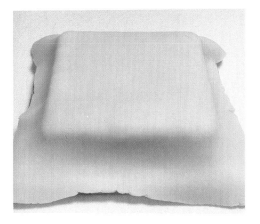

4. Centrally cover the cake with the sheet of marzipan. By rotating a flat hand on the cake-top, smooth the marzipan (and, thus, expel the trapped air).

5. Gently smooth the marzipan down each cake-side, being careful to smoothly shape the corners.

6. Trim surplus marzipan from the cake-base (by keeping the knife blade as parallel to the cake-side as possible). Leave to dry for at least 24 hours.

HOW TO MARZIPAN A PETAL (OR OTHER ROUND) SHAPED FRUIT CAKE BEFORE COVERING WITH

SUGARPASTE

BEATRICE

1. Picture showing a 9″ diameter petal shaped fruit cake on 12″ and 15″ diameter petal shaped cake boards (to indicate required proportions).

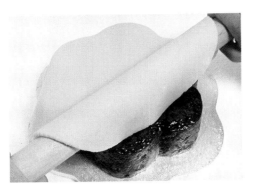

2. Position cake on the small board. Fill-in the cake imperfections with marzipan and then brush boiling apricot puree over the top and sides. Centrally cover the whole cake with a ¼″ thick sheet of marzipan.

3. Sprinkle icing sugar over the marzipan. Rotate a cake smoother (or palm of a hand) over the cake-top to smooth the marzipan and, thus, expel any trapped air.

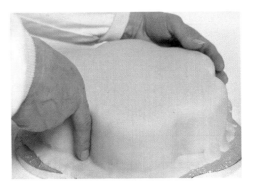

4. Gently smooth the marzipan down the cake-side and ease it into each crevice.

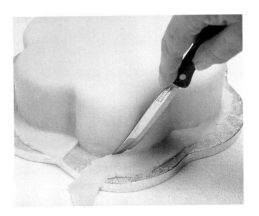

5. Trim surplus marzipan from the cake-base (by keeping the knife blade as close to the cake-side as possible).

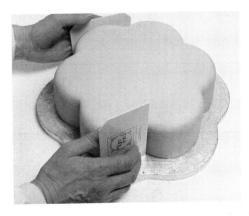

6. By steadying the cake at the rear (with a cake scraper), emphasize each crevice by gentle pressure with another cake scraper. Leave to to dry for at least 24 hours.

17

HOW TO COVER A MARZIPANNED FRUIT CAKE WITH

SUGARPASTE

AND COATING A BOARD WITH ROYAL ICING

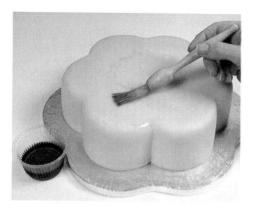

7. Brush over the marzipan with cooled boiled water or liquor of choice.

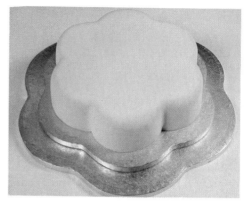

10. Align and fix the cake-boards together. Leave to dry for at least 24 hours.

8. Cover the whole cake with a thin sheet of sugarpaste. Then follow the instructions in No's. 3 and 4 on page 17.

11. Soften some royal icing (without glycerine) with water to a dropping consistency. Pipe this icing on to a part of the top cake-board (through a greaseproof paper piping bag without a piping tube).

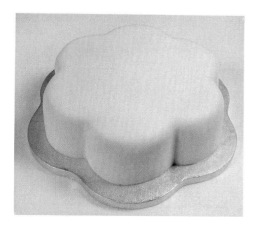

9. Follow the instructions in No's 5 and 6 on page 17 (to trim and shape the sugarpaste).

12. Immediately brush the royal icing to the edge of the board, thus ensuring a smooth overall surface.

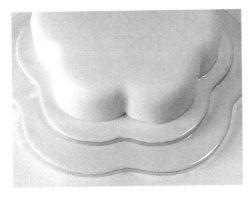

13. Repeat No's 11 and 12 until the top cake-board is complete, then repeat No's 11 and 12 in respect of the bottom board until it is also covered. Leave to dry for 24 hours.

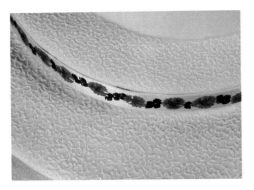

14. Fix a floral ribbon around the edge of the top cake-board. Pipe royal icing filigree on both cake-board surfaces.

15. Pipe plain shells around cake-base and at the base of the ribbon.

BEATRICE'S TEMPLATE

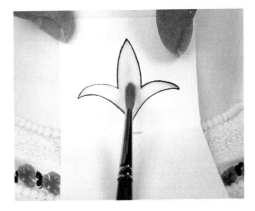

16. Cut out a paper template, using the drawing as a guide and place against the side of one of the cake sections. Brush confectioners' dusting powder inside the template. Repeat pattern around cake, as shown.

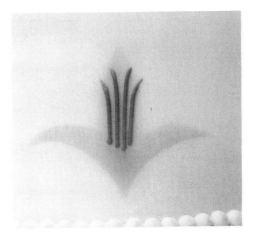

17. Pipe stamens on each pattern, as shown.

18. Pipe an anther on to each stamen and add dots to complete the floral motif.

BEATRICE

FLORAL DECORATIONS OF CHOICE,
SUGAR DOVES AND A MATCHING
RIBBON AROUND THE EDGE OF THE
BOTTOM CAKE-BOARD WILL SHOW
'BEATRICE' OFF TO PERFECTION.

HOW TO PIPE BUTTERCREAM/ ROYAL ICING SHAPES

1. SHELL. Hold piping bag at the angle shown and start to press.

2. Continue pressing, whilst lifting bag.

3. Continue pressing until shell is of required size.

4. Stop pressing, then slide tube down along surface to form tail.

1. ROPE. Pipe spring-shape in clockwise direction, using even pressure and keeping bag horizontal.

2. Continue piping in a straight even pattern. Stop piping and pull bag away in a half-turn.

1. 'C' SCROLL. Pipe in clockwise direction, increasing the size of the circle to form the body.

2. Continue piping, reducing the size of the circles, then form the tail – using reduced pressure.

1. 'S' SCROLL. Hold piping bag at angle shown and start to press.

2. Continue piping in a clockwise direction, increasing the size of each circle to form the body.

3. Continue piping, reducing the size of the circles from the centre.

4. Continue piping and form the tail by reducing pressure.

CRIMPING

1. Cover a cake with sugarpaste (in one of the ways described between pages 14 and 18) and immediately crimp the top edge – using a crimping tool of the size and pattern required.

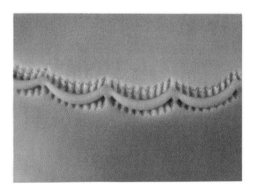

2. This picture shows the result of careful and correct crimping (through using even pressure on each crimp).

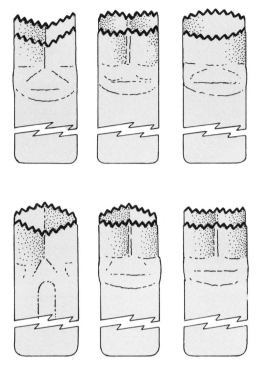

SOME SAMPLE CRIMPING TOOLS.

THIS SERIES OF INDIVIDUAL CRIMPING STYLES DEMONSTRATES THE VARIETY OF PATTERNS AVAILABLE FROM CRIMPING TOOLS. CRIMPING CAN BE ENHANCED WITH PIPED ROYAL ICING, RIBBON INSERTION AND BOWS.

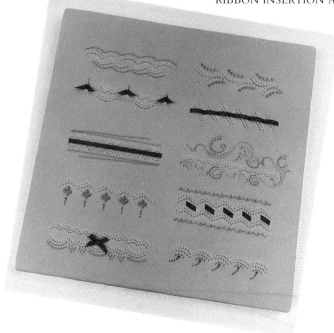

RIBBON INSERTION

1. Cut a band of paper to completely cover the cake-side(s). Design and draw the required pattern on the band (ensuring it is in proportion). Pin the band to the cake-side(s) and then cut through the pattern on the band into the cake-side.

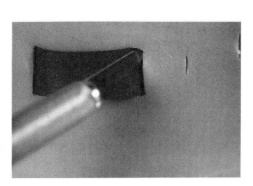

2. Remove the band and insert a piece of ribbon (of suitable length and width) into a slit in the sugarpaste. Assist the other end of the ribbon into the next slit with a sharp and pointed instrument.

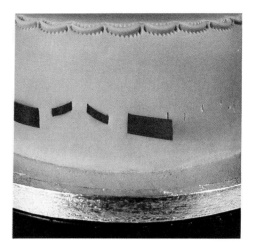

3. Repeat No. 2 to achieve a weave effect, until the pattern is complete.

NOTE: FURTHER DESIGNS ARE TO BE FOUND ON PAGE 24.

PICTURE SHOWING PATTERNS OBTAINABLE BY INSERTING THE HEADS OF CRIMPING TOOLS INTO SUGARPASTE (THUS GIVING A STITCHING EFFECT). THE 'STITCH' DESIGNS ARE DECORATED WITH PIPED ROYAL ICING, RIBBON INSERTION AND BOWS.

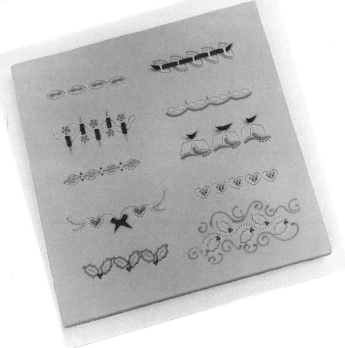

RIBBON INSERTION

Each of these designs may be used to enhance the decorative appearance of a sugarpasted cake – provided the instructions given on page 23 (1)-(3) are closely followed.

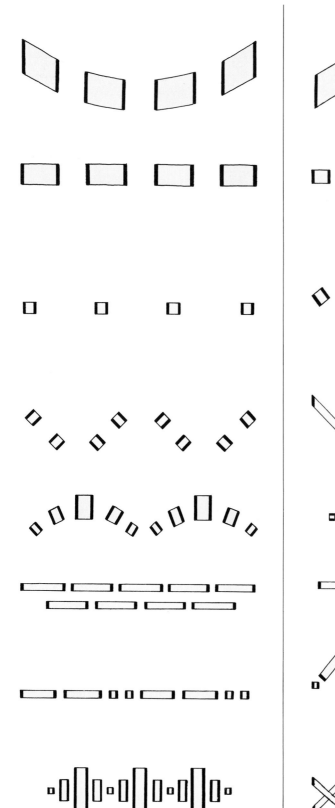
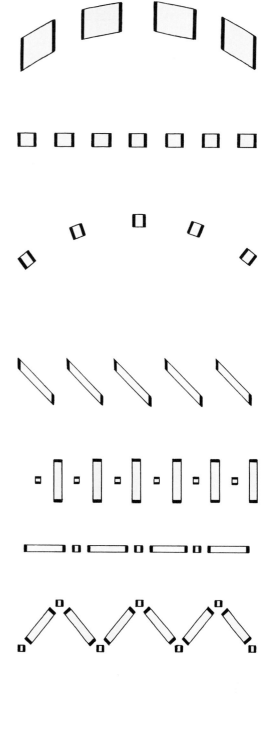

WRITING STYLES GUIDE

The following are but a few of the hundreds of writing styles available to the cake artist (from calligraphy, needlework and other craft books, as well as from Mary Ford's WRITING IN ICING BOOK).

EASY-TO-MAKE FLOWERS
POINSETTIA

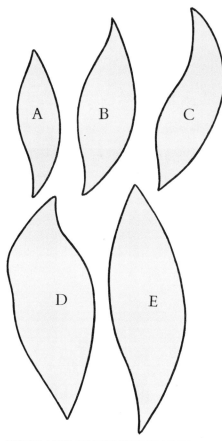

TEMPLATES OF THE FIVE LEAF SHAPES
REQUIRED FOR EACH POINSETTIA.

TO MAKE A WORKING TEMPLATE –
TRACE THE OUTLINE OF A LEAF ON
GREASEPROOF PAPER AND THEN
TRANSFER THE OUTLINE ON TO
CARD. CUT OUT THE SHAPE, WHICH
THEN BECOMES THE WORKING
TEMPLATE. A SEPARATE TEMPLATE IS
REQUIRED FOR EACH LEAF SHAPE.

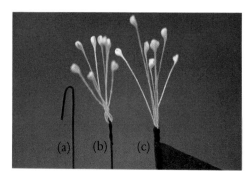

1. (a) Cut and bend (to shape shown) a length of green 24 gauge wire, to form stem.

(b) Loop four double-headed stamen wires through the stem crook and twist the wires, as shown.

(c) Wrap floral tape around the wires where shown.

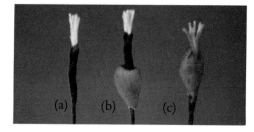

2. (a) Remove stamen heads by cutting the wires about ¼" above the tape.

(b) Mould a flower paste cone and insert the stem down through its centre.

(c) Moisten the tape above the cone (with egg white or gum arabic solution) and then remould the cone to the shape and in the position shown (to form a flower head). Leave to dry for 24 hours.

(NOTE: Seven flower heads required for the poinsettia).

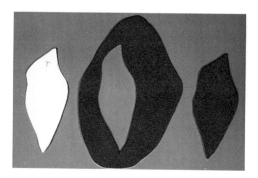

3. Roll out and cut a leaf from a sheet of flower paste – USING TEMPLATE **D.**

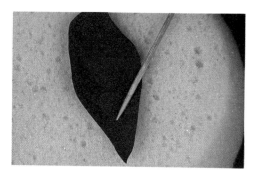

4. Immediately place the leaf on to a dry household sponge and mark the veins with light pressure from a cocktail stick.

NOTE: TO COMPLETE A POINSETTIA
THE FOLLOWING LEAVES ARE
REQUIRED
TEMPLATE **A** = 4
TEMPLATE **B** = 2
TEMPLATE **C** = 2
TEMPLATE **D** = 3
TEMPLATE **E** = 3 RED & GREEN.

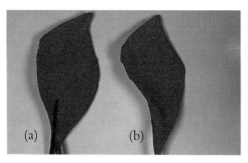

5. (a) Remove leaf from the sponge and lay a length of green 26 gauge wire on the leaf, as shown. Moisten the leaf's base (where the wire is resting) with egg white or gum arabic solution.

(b) Pinch the base of the leaf on to the wire to secure it. Leave to dry for 24 hours.

8. Tape the leaves from TEMPLATE **A** to the flower stem. Then add the leaves from TEMPLATE **B,** followed by the leaves from TEMPLATE **C.**

6. Brush the flower heads and leaves with confectioners' dusting powder, then pipe two royal icing dots on each flower head. Leave to dry for one hour.

9. Continue taping leaves to the stem from TEMPLATE **D.** Then add the red leaves from TEMPLATE **E** and complete the poinsettia by taping the green leaves from TEMPLATE **E** to the stem.

7. Secure the flower head stems with floral tape.

THE FLORAL SPRAY ILLUSTRATED ON THIS CHRISTMAS CAKE PLAQUE HAS THE POINSETTIA AS ITS CENTREPIECE. OTHER SEASONAL SUGAR FLOWERS, LEAVES, BERRIES AND NUTS, HELP ENHANCE THE SHAPE AND COLOURS OF THE POINSETTIA.

EASY-TO-MAKE FLOWERS
ROSE

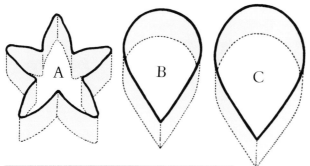

ROSE CUTTERS SHOWN (FULL SIZE)
ARE (A) THE CALYX CUTTER, (B) THE
SMALL PETAL CUTTER AND (C) THE
LARGE PETAL CUTTER.

NOTE: IN SUBSTITUTION FOR METAL
CUTTERS, TRACE THE OUTLINES ON
GREASEPROOF PAPER, THEN
TRANSFER ON TO CARD. CUT OUT
EACH SHAPE AND USE AS A
TEMPLATE.

1. (a) Cut and bend (to shape shown) a
length of lime green 24 gauge wire, to
form the stem.
(b) Mould a cone out of flower paste.
Moisten the wire crook with egg white or
gum arabic solution and insert it into the cone.
Continue moulding the cone to form the shape
shown.

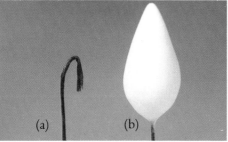

2. Roll out and cut a petal from a sheet of
flower paste, using cutter (B). Place the
petal on a dry household sponge and thin the
edge by gentle pressure with a ball-shaped (or
other suitable) tool.

4. Wrap the left side of the petal around the
cone and then the right side (ensuring the
top is left open).

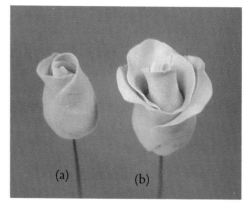

5. (a) Make – using cutter (B) – and fix two
further petals to the rose centre. This,
together with the calyx – see No's 7 and 8 –
completes the rose bud.
(b) Make – using cutter (B) – and fix four
more petals to the bud. Each petal, when being
fixed, should be shaped to give an opening
bloom effect.

3. Place the petal on a flat surface. Moisten
the cone '1(b)' and position it on the
petal, as shown.

6. Make – using cutter (C) – and fix four further petals, to complete the rose bloom. Each petal, when being fixed, should be shaped to give an open bloom effect. (NOTE: Further petals can be added to produce a larger rose).

8. Make, insert and fix a flower paste cone to the calyx. (Repeat No's. 7 and 8 to complete any rose bud made). Leave to dry for 24 hours.

7. Using cutter (A), cut a calyx from a sheet of flower paste and, after moistening its centre, fix to the base of the rose whilst shaping each calyx leaf, as shown.

9. To make the rose spray illustrated –
(a) make a variety of rose leaves – by using the instructions on Page 33 No. 7 as a guide – BUT cutting each shape from one of the rose leaf templates.
(b) Make the flower heads shown.
(c) Using floral tape, tape the rose stems and leaves together (starting from the top of the spray).
(d) Trim off surplus wire.

ROSE LEAF TEMPLATES

EASY-TO-MAKE FLOWERS
DAFFODIL

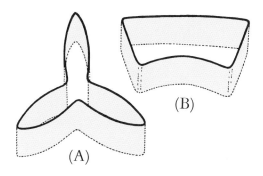

DAFFODIL CUTTERS SHOWN (FULL SIZE) ARE (A) THE PETAL CUTTER AND (B) THE TRUMPET CUTTER.

NOTE: IN SUBSTITUTION FOR METAL CUTTERS, TRACE THE OUTLINES ON GREASEPROOF PAPER, THEN TRANSFER ON TO CARD. CUT OUT EACH SHAPE AND USE AS A TEMPLATE.

3. Immediately mark each petal, as shown, with a cocktail stick.

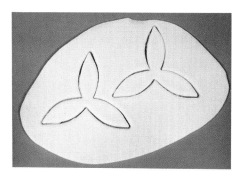

1. Roll out and cut two petal shapes from a sheet of flower paste.

4. Moisten the centre of one of the petal shapes with egg white or gum arabic solution. Then immediately join the two shapes to form a six-petalled flower. Pierce the flower centre with a cocktail stick (to make a central hole).

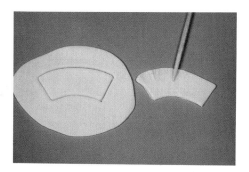

2. Place petal shapes on a dry household sponge and thin the edges by gentle pressure with a ball-shaped (or other suitable) tool.

5. Roll out a sheet of flower paste and cut the shape shown with cutter (B). Frill the longer (outer) edge by rolling a cocktail stick backwards and forwards a little at a time.

LEAF TEMPLATE

6. Moisten one end of the shape with egg white or gum arabic solution, then fold over and fix one end to the other to form the trumpet.

10. Pull the stem though the flower until the flower paste ball and stamen heads are in the position shown. Then use a cocktail stick to flatten the flower paste ball.

7. Moisten the base of the trumpet and fix to the petals, as shown. Leave to dry for 24 hours.
(NOTE: Two flowers required for the spray shown).

11. Mould a cone of flower paste and insert the stem through its centre. Moisten the base of the flower with egg white or gum arabic solution and fix the cone to it, as shown. Leave to dry for 24 hours.

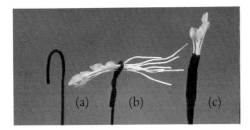

8. (a) Cut and bend (to shape shown) a length of lime green 24 gauge wire, to form the stem.
(b) Loop six single stamens through the wire stem and twist the stem to secure them.
(c) Turn stamen heads to the upright position and tape them to the stem with floral tape.

12. Wind white floral tape around the stem (in the length and shape shown) and coat with confectioners' dusting powder.

9. Mould a ball of flower paste and insert the stem through it. Moisten the inside centre of the flower and insert the stem through the existing hole.

13. Cut out and mark two flower paste leaves (using the Leaf Template as a guide). Insert a length of 26 gauge wire into the base of each leaf and then leave to dry for 24 hours. Place the wired leaves against the flower stems and fix together by wrapping with floral tape.

EASY-TO-MAKE FLOWERS
CHRYSANTHEMUM

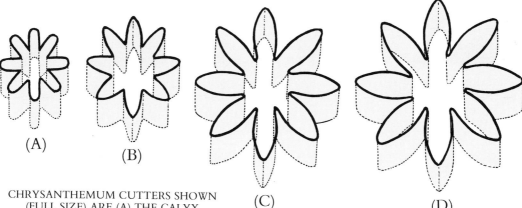

(A) (B) (C) (D)

CHRYSANTHEMUM CUTTERS SHOWN (FULL SIZE) ARE (A) THE CALYX CUTTER, (B) THE 1ST INTERNAL PETAL CUTTER, (C) THE 2ND INTERNAL PETAL CUTTER, AND (D) THE EXTERNAL PETAL CUTTER.

NOTE: IN SUBSTITUTION FOR METAL CUTTERS, TRACE THE OUTLINES ON GREASEPROOF PAPER, THEN TRANSFER ON TO CARD. CUT OUT EACH SHAPE AND USE AS A TEMPLATE.

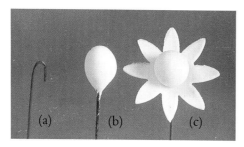

1. (a) Cut and bend (to shape shown) a length of lime green 24 gauge wire.
(b) Mould a piece of flower paste to form a ball. Moisten the bent end of the wire with egg white or gum arabic solution and insert it into the ball.
(c) Roll out and cut a ring of petals from a sheet of flower paste, using cutter (B). Moisten its centre and then thread '(b)' through it. (NOTE: Always moisten the centre of each petal ring – with egg white or gum arabic solution – when fixing to flower head).

2. (a) Immediately fold the petals around the ball.
(b) Repeat '1(c)' to add another ring of petals.
(c) Immediately fold the petals around the flower-head.

3. (a) Roll out and cut a ring of petals from a sheet of flower paste, using cutter (C).
(b) Cut each petal in half, as shown, to make 16 petals.
(c) Curl each petal by rolling a cocktail stick gently backwards and forwards.
(d) Picture showing the completed ring of petals.

4. (a) Immediately thread the ring of petals on to the flower head.
(b) Fold petals around the flower head, as shown.
(c) Repeat '3.(a) – (c)' twice more (to increase the size of the flower-head).

5. Using Cutter (D), repeat '3(a)-(c)' and '4.(a) and (b)' three times. (This completes the chrysanthemum flower head).

(a)   (b)

6. (a) Using cutter (A), cut a calyx from a sheet of flower paste and after moistening its centre, fix to the back of the flower head.
(b) Gently spread each calyx leaf to the back of the flower head with finger pressure. Leave to dry for 24 hours.

(a)   (b)

(c)   (d)

7. (a) Roll out and cut a flower paste leaf in the shape shown.
(b) Smooth out the leaf's edges with a ball-shaped (or other suitable) tool.
(c) Insert 26 gauge lime green wire through the leaf's base (for about ⅓rd of the leaf's length).
(d) Highlight the leaf with confectioners' dusting powder.

8. Highlight the flower centre with confectioners' dusting powder (by using a clean, fine and soft artist's brush).

9. Thicken the flower stem by wrapping it in floral tape.

10. Place the wired leaf against the flower stem and fix together by wrapping with floral tape. Add further flowers and leaves to the main stem by this method. Then trim off surplus wire.

EASY-TO-MAKE FLOWERS
SWEET PEA

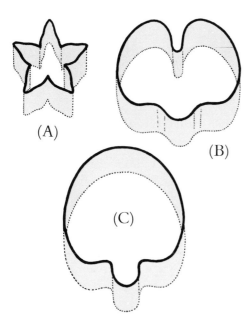

(A)

(B)

(C)

SWEET PEA CUTTERS SHOWN (FULL SIZE) ARE (A) THE CALYX CUTTER, (B) THE INTERNAL PETAL CUTTER AND (C) THE EXTERNAL PETAL CUTTER.

NOTE: IN SUBSTITUTION FOR METAL CUTTERS, TRACE THE OUTLINES ON GREASEPROOF PAPER, THEN TRANSFER ON TO CARD. CUT OUT EACH SHAPE AND USE AS A TEMPLATE.

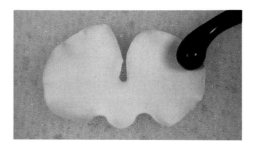

3. Place the first shape on to a dry household sponge and thin the edge by gentle pressure with a ball-shaped (or other suitable) tool.

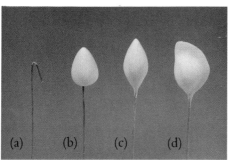

(a) (b) (c) (d)

1. (a) Cut and bend (to shape shown) a length of lime green 26 gauge wire.
(b) Mould a piece of flower paste to form a cone. Moisten the end of the wire with egg white or gum arabic solution and insert into the cone.
(c) Mould the base of the cone to the shape shown.
(d) Pinch one side of the cone to form a pasty shape (which becomes the centre of the flower).

4. Moisten the centre of the petal with egg white or gum arabic solution and fix it around the flower centre.
(This, with the addition of the calyx – see No. 8 – completes the sweet pea bud).

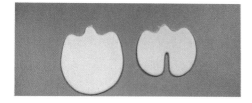

2. Roll out and cut the two petal shapes shown from a sheet of flower paste (and cover with polythene to prevent the paste drying).

5. Frill the edge of the second petal by rolling a cocktail stick backwards and forwards a little at a time.

6. Immediately fix (with egg white or gum arabic solution) the second petal to the flower head by gently curving it from behind. Pinch the centre 'tongue' (at the base of the petal) on to the wire stem. Leave to dry for 48 hours in an upright position.

8. Using cutter (A), cut the flower calyx from a sheet of flower paste. Pinch the edges of the calyx, moisten its centre (with egg white or gum arabic solution) then fix to the base of the flower (by pushing the wire stem through the centre).
This picture illustrates a sweet pea bud and a sweet pea in full bloom.

7. Highlight the flower centre and petal edges with confectioners' dusting powder (by using a clean, fine and soft artist's brush). (NOTE: The shade of confectioners' dusting powder can be lightened by the addition of cornflour).

9. Curl lengths of 26 gauge lime green wire to form tendrils and then fix around sweet pea stems.

A CAKE OF THIS DESIGN ENHANCES THE FLORAL SWEET PEA DECORATION.

EASY-TO-MAKE FLOWERS
CARNATION

THE CARNATION CUTTER SHOWN IS
ACTUAL SIZE.

NOTE: IN SUBSTITUTION FOR METAL
CUTTER, TRACE THE OUTLINE ON
GREASEPROOF PAPER, THEN
TRANSFER ON TO CARD. CUT OUT
THE SHAPE AND USE AS A TEMPLATE.

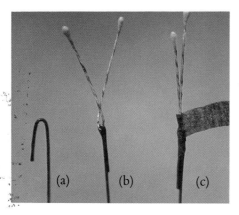

(a) (b) (c)

1. (a) Cut and bend (to shape shown) a
length of green 24 gauge wire, to form
the stem.
(b) Loop a double-headed stamen wire
through the wire hook and secure by twisting
the stem.
(c) Now use floral tape to conceal the
join.

2. Using the carnation cutter, cut a disc
from a sheet of flower paste. Immediately
frill the edge by gently rolling a cocktail stick
backwards and forwards.

3. Moisten the centre of the disc with egg
white or gum arabic solution (ensuring
the frill edge remains dry). Then push the stem
through the disc's centre and fold the disc over
(to cover the join of the wires). Cut off the
stamen heads.

(a) (b)

4. (a) Moisten the right-hand centre of the
flower head and gently fold that side
over, as shown.
(b) Turn the flower over and repeat (a),
which now forms the carnation's centre.

5. Repeat No. 2, then moisten the disc's
centre. Push the flower stem through the
disc, as before and gently wrap the disc around
the flower head.

6. Repeat No. 5. This completes the carnation bloom (although, by personal choice, additional discs can be added – to create a larger flower head). Leave to dry for 24 hours.

LEAF TEMPLATE

7. Trim off protruding stamen wires. Dust the carnation with confectioners' dusting powder – in colour of choice (by using a clean, fine and soft artist's brush).
NOTE: If a carnation with leaves is required –
   (a) Cut out the leaf shapes from a sheet of flower paste.
   (b) Insert wire into each leaf – by following the instructions on Page 33 No. 7.
   (c) Tape the carnation stem, as shown on Page 33 No. 9.
   (d) Complete the flower, by joining the leaves to the stem, as shown on Page 33 No. 10.

PICTURE ILLUSTRATING THE USE OF CARNATION BLOOMS IN CONJUNCTION WITH OTHER FLOWERS, FLOWER BUDS AND RIBBON, TO CREATE A BEAUTIFUL CAKE OR TABLE CENTRE-PIECE.

EASY-TO-MAKE
SIMPLE FLOWERS

SAMPLE A

1. Make a cone from flower paste, then insert the pointed end of a wooden skewer into its base.

2. Use a craft knife to cut the bottom half of the cone into six equal sections. Remove the skewer.

3. (a) Hold the cone and pinch each section between finger and thumb, to form the petals shown in (b).

4. (a) Cut and bend (to shape shown), a length of green 28 gauge wire and insert it through the centre of the flower.
(b) Moisten the wire crook with egg white or gum arabic solution, then pull it into the flower head until just visible. Leave to dry for 24 hours.
Brush the flower with confectioners' dusting powder.

SAMPLE B

This picture illustrates a token sample of simple flowers (which can be made in many shapes and sizes just by following the above guidelines). Such flowers are very simple to make and may be used for many purposes.

SAMPLE C

(a)   (b)   (c)

1. Follow the instructions in SAMPLE A, No's. 1–3 to produce (a), then –
(b) roll a cocktail stick backwards and forwards over each petal.
(c) Follow the instructions in SAMPLE A, No. 4 (a) and (b).

2. Picture showing completed flower.

EASY-TO-MAKE FLOWERS
FREESIA

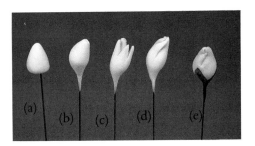

1. (a) Cut and bend a length of green 28 gauge wire into a crook shape. Moisten the crook with egg white or gum arabic solution and insert into moulded cone-shaped flower paste.

(b) Now mould the cone to the shape shown.

(c) Cut a cross into the top of the cone with a pair of scissors.

(d) Twist the top a quarter of a turn.

(e) Paint the bud's calyx with edible food colouring. Leave to dry for 24 hours. (NOTE: Four buds required for the completed spray illustrated).

2. To make an open freesia flower, follow the instructions on Page 38, SAMPLE A No's. 1-3 and then place the flower on to a dry household sponge. Spread each petal by gentle pressure with a ball-shaped (or other suitable) tool.

3. Cut and bend a length of green 26 gauge wire into a crook shape. Moisten the crook with egg white or gum arabic solution and insert into the flower head until just visible.

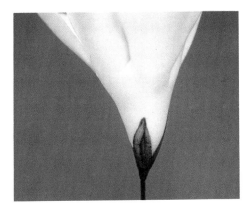

4. Paint the flower's calyx with edible food colouring. Leave to dry for 24 hours. (NOTE: Three flowers required for the completed spray illustrated).

5. Wind floral tape around the top of one bud stem, then add the second bud stem and tape it to the first. Continue in this manner until all bud stems are taped together. Then add and tape each flower stem in the same manner.

6. Mould and fix (with egg white or gum arabic solution) a small ball of flower paste to the centre of each flower. Cut twelve stamen wires and insert (with tweezers) four into each flower paste ball. (NOTE: The stamen heads should not protrude above the flower heads). Brush each flower with confectioners' dusting powder. To complete the spray, bend the wires to the shape shown.

EASY-TO-MAKE FLOWERS
LILY

THE CUTTER SHOWN (ACTUAL SIZE) IS PART OF AN *ORCHID CUTTER SET* WHICH IS USED TO PRODUCE A LILY PETAL.

NOTE: IN SUBSTITUTION FOR METAL CUTTER, TRACE THE OUTLINE ON GREASEPROOF PAPER, THEN TRANSFER ON TO CARD. CUT OUT THE SHAPE AND USE AS A TEMPLATE.

1. (a) Roll out and cut a petal from a sheet of flower paste and place on a dry household sponge.
(b) Thin the edge by gently pressing with a ball–shaped (or other suitable) tool.

2. (a) Insert 28 gauge green wire through the petal's base (for about ⅓rd of the petal's length).
(b) Immediately fold the petal over a length of 1″ diameter dowel. Leave to dry for 24 hours.
(NOTE: Six petals will be required for each lily flower).

3. Brush each petal with confectioner's dusting powder (thick at the base and gradually thinning towards the top, as shown).

4. Add the lily spots with a finely pointed artist's brush (using edible food colouring).

5. (a) Cut and bend (to the shape shown) a length of 26 gauge green wire.
(b) Mould a piece of flower paste to form a cone. Moisten the bent end of the wire with egg white or gum arabic solution and insert into the cone.
(c) Mould the base of the cone to the shape shown.

10. Bind together (with floral tape) three petals to the stamens, as shown.

6. Mark the flower paste with a cocktail stick, to create the closed bud effect shown.
Leave to dry for 24 hours.

7. Using a soft, thick artist's brush, dust confectioners' dusting powder over the bud.

11. To complete the lily, bind (with floral tape) the three remaining petals to the stem, as shown.

8. Mould sugar paste stamen heads on to the tip of 28 gauge lime green wire and then cut to length (approximately 4 inches). Six stamens required for each lily.
(NOTE: Upright stamens denote young flowers and bent stamens denote mature flowers).

9. Bind six stamen stems together with floral tape.

12. This picture illustrates a single lily spray displaying two open lilies and two buds (bound together with floral tape).

IMPORTANT NOTICE
*Before decorating any cake it is essential to read the whole
sequence of instructions and, please, ensure the necessary
materials and equipment, as well as sufficient time, are available
to complete the cake. (A pictorial reference to all the cakes is to be
found on pages 6 and 7 and recipes and basic information are on
pages 8 to 25).*

DELORA

1. Place a coated cake on to a doyley and board. Fix a narrow ribbon around cake-base.

3. Using a trowel shaped palette knife, thinly spread royal icing over the doyley (ensuring the doyley doesn't move).

2. Carefully select a well patterned plastic doyley and place it on the cake-top.

4. Immediately lift one edge of the doyley and peel off with a steady continuous movement.

5. Carefully inspect the doyley pattern on the cake-top (and, if necessary, pipe-in any defects).

6. Pipe floral motifs around cake-side, as shown. Complete cake-top with a sugar flower.

ZOE

ZOE'S TEMPLATE

3. Pipe-in the shoes, remaining part of the petticoat and the dress bodice. Leave to dry for 10 minutes.

1. Place and fix waxed paper over Zoe's template. Pipe-in face (ensuring the cheeks and nose are thick and the eyes thin). Then pipe-in the arms and legs. Leave to dry for 10 minutes.

4. Pipe-in the remaining parts of the dress. Leave to dry for 12 hours.

2. Pipe-in hair (ensuring a wavy effect is obtained – by twirling the icing bag whilst piping). Then pipe-in the socks and parts of the dress and petticoat shown. Leave to dry for 10 minutes.

5. Complete Zoe's clothes with piped dots and bows, as shown. Pipe hair bow. Paint-in the hair and face features shown (using edible food colourings). Leave to dry for 12 hours in a warm dry atmosphere.

6. Roll out a thin sheet of sugarpaste and, using a blossom cutter, cut one flower from the sheet. Use a ball-shaped modelling tool to press the flower into a dry sponge (to obtain a dish shape). Remove flower and leave to dry for 12 hours (Approximately 80 flowers of various sizes required).

7. Brush confectioners' dusting powder (of the required colour) into the centre of each flower. Pipe a royal icing bulb into each flower.

8. Place coated sponge on to a doyley and board and then pipe shells around cake-base. Divide cake-side into eight and fix flowers to form the garlands shown. (NOTE: A guide to dividing the cake-side is given on Page 76 No. 1).

9. Carefully remove Zoe from the waxed paper and fix to the cake-top in the position shown.

10. Fix flowers around Zoe, as shown. Pipe-in grass.

11. Pipe name of choice on cake-top in royal icing and decorate in the manner shown.

BEFORE COMMENCING THIS CAKE, PLEASE REFER TO THE *IMPORTANT NOTICE* ON PAGE 42.

ZOE

SECRET LOVE

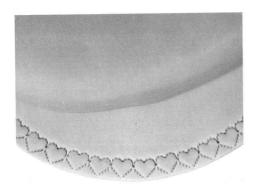

1. Place a heart-shaped cake on a round board and cover both with sugar paste. Immediately *press* a heart-shaped crimper into the sugarpaste to form a ring of hearts around the cake-board edge.

3. Pipe in a variety of curved lines around the cake-top, as shown, then pipe a series of dots to complete decoration.

2. Pipe plain shells around cake-base. Fix a prepared floral spray to the cake-top in the position shown.

4. Pipe inscription of choice and then underline and decorate in complimentary colours. Fix ribbon and bows around cake-side (in matching colour to the spray ribbon).

BEFORE COMMENCING THIS CAKE, PLEASE REFER TO THE *IMPORTANT NOTICE* ON PAGE 42.

KERRY

KERRY'S TEMPLATE

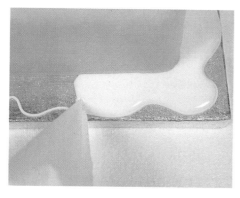

1. Place the coated cake on to the centre of a square cake-board. Pipe a royal icing wavy line around cake-board and flood-in the area between the line and cake-base with soft royal icing. Leave to dry for 24 hours.

2. Roll out a sheet of sugarpaste and, using a veiner, press to obtain leaf veins. Keeping the veins central, cut out the leaf with a leaf cutter. Curl leaf to required shape. Leave to dry for 12 hours. (14 various sized leaves required).

4. Pipe the owl's body (in royal icing) on to the branch and immediately brush – using downward strokes – to form feathers.

3. Pipe the branch shown (in royal icing) on to the cake-top.

5. Pipe-in the wings and again brush to form feathers.

48

6. Pipe-in the head, keeping the eye sockets shallow. Then pipe-in the eye balls.

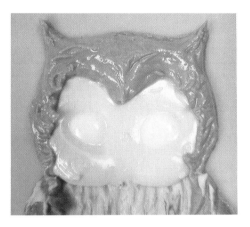

7. Pipe-in the head feathers and ears, then brush as before. Pipe-in talons.
Leave to dry for 12 hours.

8. Paint-in facial features with edible food colouring.
(NOTE: To avoid colour spreading, mix the colour with an equal amount of clear alcohol).
Form and fix a sugarpaste beak.

9. Fix the prepared leaves to the branch. Make and fix some sugarpaste stars in the positions shown.

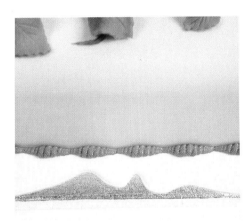

10. Pipe barrel scrolls around cake-base to complete the cake.

BEFORE COMMENCING THIS CAKE, PLEASE REFER TO THE *IMPORTANT NOTICE* ON PAGE 42.

CHRYSTAL

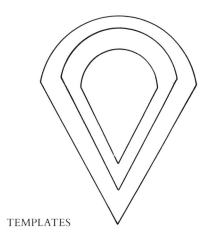

TEMPLATES

1. Cover cake and board with sugarpaste. Divide cake-top edge into six equal portions with piped dots. Trace the template on to a thin sheet of paper and cut out shape. Using the template as a guide, pipe the design between each dot, as shown. Pipe a curved line on the cake-board, immediately below each design.

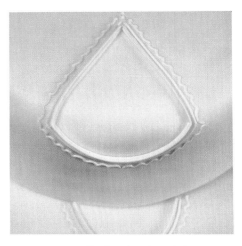

2. Pipe a smaller line beside and then on top of each piped line. Pipe a scalloped line beside each piped design.

3. Pipe plain bulbs between each cake-board piped design.

4. Pipe a left and right 'C' scroll at each cake-top piped dot, as shown.

5. Pipe small shells around the cake-base inside each cake-board piped design. Pipe a line over each cake-base bulb.

6. Overpipe each 'C' scroll with a smaller tube.

BEFORE COMMENCING THIS CAKE, PLEASE REFER TO THE *IMPORTANT NOTICE* ON PAGE 42.

7. Pipe equally spaced 'C' scrolls around the cake-board edge.

8. Fix artificial flowers and leaves to the cake-base and top.

NOTE: THIS CAKE DESIGN CAN BE
EASILY ADAPTED TO PRODUCE
MULTI-TIERED CAKES, AS DESCRIBED
ON THE NEXT PAGE

CHRYSTAL

Chrystal is a lovely, dignified and relatively easy-to-decorate cake which is eminently suitable as a one, two or three-tiered wedding cake.

WEDDING CAKE GUIDELINES

1. Only use a well tried quality recipe for the cake(s).

2. During the maturing period, do not add too much alcohol to the cake (as this may work through the marzipan and discolour the sugarpaste).

3. Plan well ahead –
(a) When preparing the cake mixture, ensure there is sufficient for the number of tiers required and the size of each tier.
(b) The cake(s) should be made at least 8 weeks before the wedding.
(c) Marzipan the cake(s) four weeks before the wedding.
(d) Complete coating and decorating the cake(s) one week before the wedding.
(e) On average, each pound of decorated wedding cake will serve six-eight people. In cases where a large distribution of wedding cake is required, separately prepared slabs of coated cake can be cut at the wedding for this purpose.
(f) Should the top tier need to be a sponge cake, use the genoese recipe on page 9 and make it ten days before the wedding. Marzipan and decorate within four days of the wedding.

4. Although it is usual to see a white cake as the centre-piece of a wedding reception, discreet colours can be used to match the general colour theme (e.g. the bridesmaids flowers and/or dresses).

5. The completed wedding cake should be kept in cardboard boxes in a dry warm atmosphere and away from direct sunlight.

6. Do not attempt to tier the cake until the wedding day reception.

7. A wedding cake should be transported with each tier in a separate box, either in the boot or on the floor of the car (DO NOT place on seats).

8. Always cut a genoese sponge cake with a dampened knife.

9. Storage –
(a) Decorated genoese sponge wedding cake should not be stored.
(b) A cut fruit cake should be sealed in waxed paper and stored in a cardboard box in a cool, *dry* atmosphere.
(c) An uncut fruit cake should be stored in a cardboard box in a cool, *dry* atmosphere.

HOW TO SUPPORT A TIERED SUGARPASTE COATED CAKE

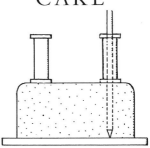

1. Place a pillar in position on cake-top. Push a skewer through the pillar and cake to the cake-board. Mark skewer at the top of the pillar, remove skewer and cut to size. Repeat for each supporting pillar.

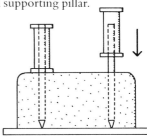

2. Replace skewer and pillars.

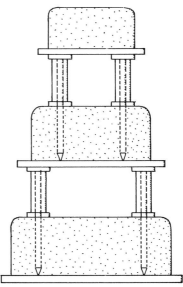

3. Assemble cake when required (see note 6).

EDWINA

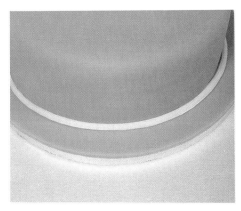

1. Cover the cake and board in sugarpaste. Pipe in a line around the cake base. Leave to dry for 30 minutes.

2. Using a star tube, pipe overlapping 'S' scrolls around cake-top edge.

3. Using a star tube, pipe overlapping 'S' scrolls over the cake-base line.

4. Overpipe each scroll (using a smaller tube). Overpipe each scroll again (using an even smaller tube). Pipe a curved rope line on cake-top, side and board, as shown.

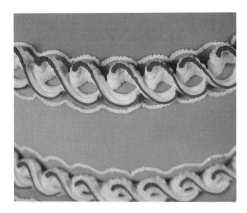

5. Overpipe each scroll (with a smaller tube) and then decorate cake-top with suitably inscribed sugarpaste book and diary. Complete the cake with sugar flowers, dots and a board-edge ribbon.

BEFORE COMMENCING THIS CAKE, PLEASE REFER TO THE *IMPORTANT NOTICE* ON PAGE 42.

RHIAN

1. Trace and cut out the template from card. Using the template as a guide, pipe the curved lines shown around cake-top. Fix a flower and leaves of choice to cake-top centre.

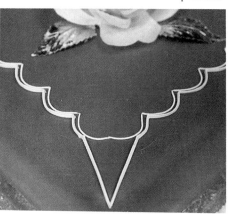

2. Pipe additional lines around cake-top, as indicated.

3. Fix a narrow ribbon around cake-side and then pipe plain shells around cake-base. Pipe a line over each shell.

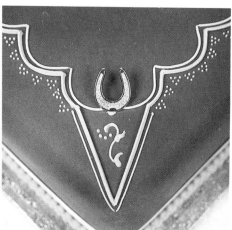

4. Decorate the cake-top with piped dots, floral motifs and lines and fix an artificial horseshoe to each cake-top corner.

RHIAN'S TEMPLATE
(FOR 8″ SQUARE CAKE)

BEFORE COMMENCING THIS CAKE, PLEASE REFER TO THE *IMPORTANT NOTICE* ON PAGE 42.

RHIAN

TREACLE

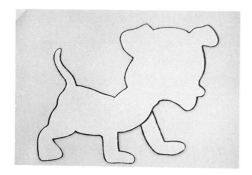

1. Trace Treacle's template on to thin card and cut around outline. Place the template on the cake-top.

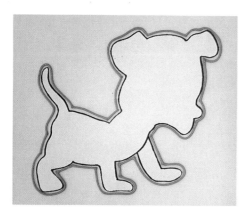

2. Pipe a line around the outside edge of the template. Leave to dry for 10 minutes. Carefully remove template.

3. Pipe-in the feature lines.

4. Pipe-in the eyes, nose and tongue.

5. Pipe inscription of choice and grass around Treacle's feet.

TEMPLATE OF TREACLE

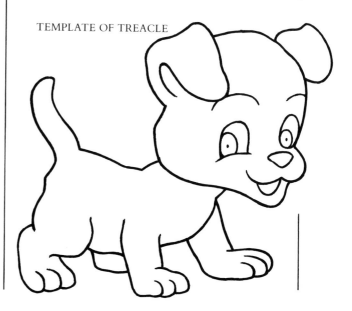

BEFORE COMMENCING THIS CAKE, PLEASE REFER TO THE *IMPORTANT NOTICE* ON PAGE 42.

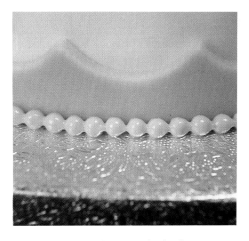

6. Roll out, cut and fix a sugarpaste scalloped band to cake-side.

7. Pipe plain shells around cake-base to complete the cake.

DEIRDRE

1. Cover each cake with sugar paste and place on its respective cake-board. Pipe 16 matching curved lines on each cake-board and flood-in with royal icing. Leave to dry for 24 hours.

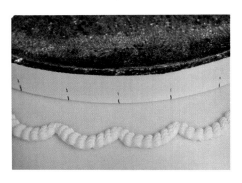

2. Divide and mark each cake-top edge into 32 divisions. (NOTE: This can be done by – (a) placing a cake board, which is slightly smaller than the cake, on the cake-top; (b) measure the circumference of the board; (c) cut a strip of paper to the size of the circumference of the board; (d) mark the paper into 32 equal divisions; then (e) fix the paper to the edge of the board, as shown). Pipe 32 matching royal icing curved rope lines around the cake-top edge.

3. Pipe 32 matching curved rope lines on the cake-board runout, as shown.

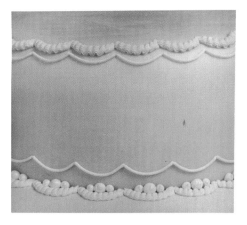

4. Pipe parallel curved lines around cake-side and then pipe bulbs around cake-base, as shown.

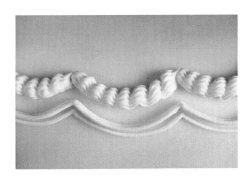

5. Pipe a thinner line under each cake-side top curved line. Then overpipe each upper curved line with a smaller tube.

6. Pipe a thinner line above each cake-side base curved line. Then overpipe each lower curved line with a smaller tube.

BEFORE COMMENCING THIS CAKE, PLEASE REFER TO THE *IMPORTANT NOTICE* ON PAGE 42.

7. Pipe lines and dots to form 8 fan shapes around cake-side. Fix a flower of choice to the top of each fan.

8. Pipe graduated dots on each cake-board curve. Fix 8 flowers around each cake-base. Add finishing touch with floral decoration.

JANINE

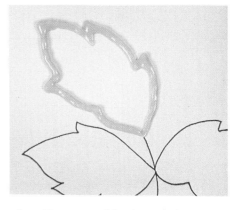

A. Trace part of the above design on to a piece of greaseproof paper. Then pipe a line over a leaf outline.

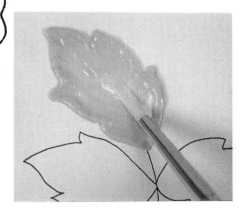

B. Immediately brush the line towards the centre of the leaf (using a slightly moistened clean brush). This should be repeatedly practiced to obtain a light transparent film of icing at the centre of the leaf (or flower). Leave for one hour.

C. Pipe leaf veins to complete each leaf.

JANINE'S TEMPLATE

BRUSH EMBROIDERY PRACTICE

NOTE: SOFT FRESHLY MADE ROYAL ICING CAN BE USED FOR ALL BRUSH EMBROIDERY (ALTHOUGH FOR MORE COMPLICATED WORK, THE FOLLOWING RECIPE IS RECOMMENDED – MIX THREE TABLESPOONS OF ROYAL ICING WITH A QUARTER-TEASPOON OF CLEAR PIPING JELLY).

BEFORE COMMENCING THIS CAKE, PLEASE REFER TO THE *IMPORTANT NOTICE* ON PAGE 42.

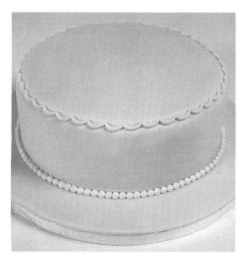

1. Cover a round cake and board with sugarpaste. Immediately crimp the cake-top edge. Then pipe royal icing bulbs around the cake-base. Leave to dry for three days.

2. Trace Janine's template on to greaseproof paper and, whilst holding it firmly in position, scribe the design (using a pointed tool) on to the cake top. Now use the BRUSH EMBROIDERY PRACTICE techniques (on page 60) to create the pattern shown. Leave to dry for one hour.

3. Pipe royal icing bulbs, lines and dots to represent flower centres and stamens.

4. Pipe a line over each cake-base bulb, then fix ribbon around cake-side.

5. Pipe inscription of choice on cake-top and decorate, as shown.

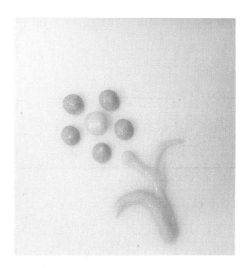

6. Pipe the repetitious floral design around the cake-board and edge. Fix ribbon to cake-board side.

JANINE

VERITY

1. Pipe a royal icing line around the cake-base. Leave to dry 30 minutes.

2. Divide the line into twelve equal sections, then pipe an 'S' scroll in each section.

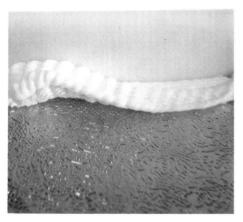

3. Overpipe each scroll (with a smaller tube).

4. Overpipe each scroll (with a smaller tube). Leave to dry for 24 hours.

5. Scratch the side of the cake – above each scroll – with a sharp implement, using a paper template of the size and shape shown.

6. Pipe suspended vertical lines from a scratch line to the top of a scroll (USING ROYAL ICING WITHOUT GLYCERINE).

BEFORE COMMENCING THIS CAKE, PLEASE REFER TO THE *IMPORTANT NOTICE* ON PAGE 42.

7. Repeat No. 6 for each scratch line. Leave to dry for one hour.

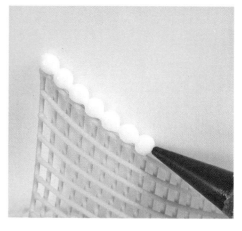

10. Pipe small plain shells along the top edges of the lattice-work.

8. Pipe across the suspended lines to form lattice-work.

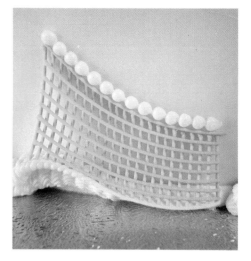

11. Overpipe each scroll with a smaller tube.

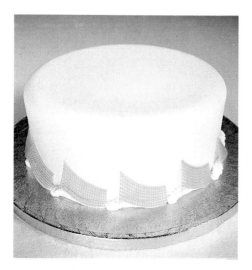

9. Picture showing completed lattice-work.

12. Pipe inscription of choice on cake-top. Fix flowers and decorations in position shown.

VERITY

CHRISTMAS ROSE

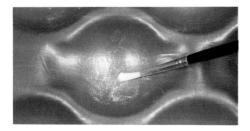

1. Dust the centre of a suitable mould (e.g. a smooth apple tray) with cornflour.

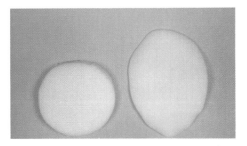

2. Cut out a thin disc of sugarpaste and then immediately flatten the edge (by tapping with a finger). This forms a petal. Five petals required for each flower.

3. Lightly moisten each petal overlap with water and interlock the five petals in the mould, as shown.

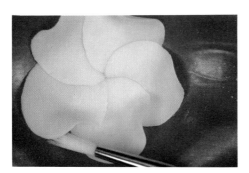

4. Curl each petal to the desired shape (using a cornflour dusted paint brush). Nine flowers required. Leave to dry for 24 hours.

5. Brush confectioners' dusting powder from the centre of the flower outwards.

6. Pipe stamens to the centre of each Christmas rose.

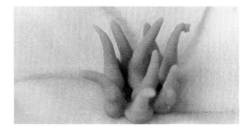

7. Pipe an anther on to each stamen. Leave to dry for 12 hours.

8. Carefully remove each Christmas rose from its mould and leave to thoroughly dry on a sheet of greaseproof paper.

9. Roll out, cut and place sugarpaste holly leaves on to a rounded mould (e.g. a dowel). Fifty leaves of varying sizes required. Leave to dry for 24 hours.

10. Roll out and fix a sugarpaste rope around cake-base. Immediately mark the rope with a tooth shaped modelling tool (to form tree bark effect).

11. Make and fix sugarpaste 'shoots' to the rope (to form a continuous tree branch).

12. Brush some softened royal icing along the branch (to create snow effect).

13. Fix the Christmas roses to the cake-top centre.

14. Paint veins on to the prepared holly leaves and fix to cake-top, as shown.

BEFORE COMMENCING THIS CAKE, PLEASE REFER TO THE *IMPORTANT NOTICE* ON PAGE 42.

15. Pipe groups of royal icing berries where shown.

16. Fix remaining holly leaves along the tree branch. Pipe berries amongst the holly leaves. Secure ribbon to cake-board edge.

SNOWBAND

1. Cover a petal shaped cake with sugarpaste and place on a round board. Stipple board with royal icing.

2. Form and fix a sugarpaste cone to the top of a flower nail and immediately snip the cone to form a Christmas tree. (One large and six small trees required).

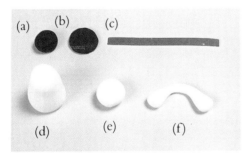

3. Roll out, cut and form the sugarpaste shapes –
(a) hat crown; (d) body;
(b) hat rim; (e) head; and
(c) scarf; (f) arms.

BEFORE COMMENCING THIS CAKE, PLEASE REFER TO THE *IMPORTANT NOTICE* ON PAGE 42.

4. Immediately fix the shapes to make a snowman. (Six snowmen required). Decorate each snowman with piped royal icing, as shown.

5. Fix the large tree to a sugarpaste tub and fix centrally on cake-top. Fix snowmen and remaining trees as shown. Brush royal icing 'snow' on the trees.

6. Pipe a message of choice on the side of each petal. Link each snowman with a narrow ribbon and then fix a ribbon to cake-board edge.

ANNAMARIE

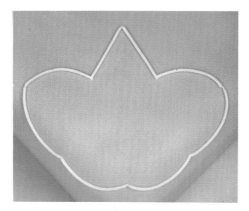

1. Cover each cake and board with sugarpaste. Trace the large template 'A' on to a thin sheet of paper. Cut out template and place against a bottom tier cake corner whilst piping a royal icing line around its edge. Repeat for each corner of each cake (using template 'B' for the middle tier and 'C' for the top tier).

3. Pipe filigree inside each template pattern.

2. Using a smaller tube, pipe a line outside each template line and then overpipe each template line. With an even smaller tube, pipe a line outside each existing line and then overpipe the inner lines.

4. Pipe plain shells along each cake-base side.

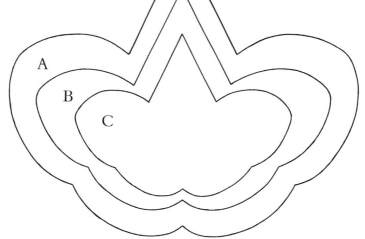

ACTUAL SIZE TEMPLATES

70

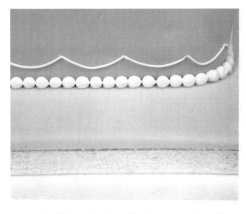

5. Divide each cake-side into equal portions (with a piped dot) and then pipe the curved lines shown.

7. Pipe a floral motif on each cake-side top edge and then join piped bird motifs with graduated dots.

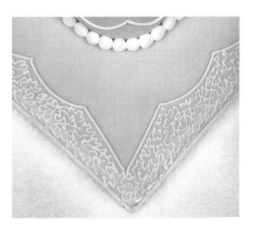

6. Pipe a 'V' line on each cake-board corner. Join each corner 'V' line with equally spaced curved lines. Pipe filigree between the piped lines and each cake-board edge.

8. Make and fix floral arrangements of choice to each tier, as shown. Complete each tier by adding artificial horseshoes and board-edge ribbon.

BEFORE COMMENCING THIS CAKE, PLEASE REFER TO THE *IMPORTANT NOTICE* ON PAGE 42.

M U M

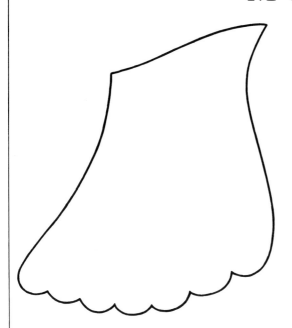

MUM'S PINAFORE TEMPLATE

3. Decorate the pinafore with piped dots in the patterns shown and then pipe an initial of choice on the pocket.

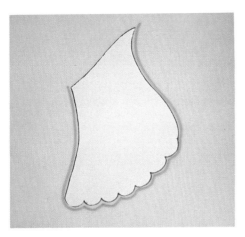

1. Trace the pinafore template on to greaseproof paper and then cut out the shape from a piece of card. Place the card pinafore on the cake-top and pipe the outline in royal icing.

4. Pipe floral motif dots on the ties.

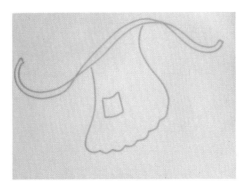

2. Remove the card and pipe the pinafore ties and pocket, as shown.

5. Pipe name of choice on cake-top and decorate with lines and dots.

BEFORE COMMENCING THIS CAKE, PLEASE REFER TO THE *IMPORTANT NOTICE* ON PAGE 42.

6. Pipe plain shells around cake-base.

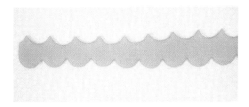

7. Roll out a sheet of sugarpaste and, using a scalloped cutter, cut a band of sugarpaste to the design shown.

8. Using a tooth-shaped modelling tool, lightly press along the length of the bottom half of the band.

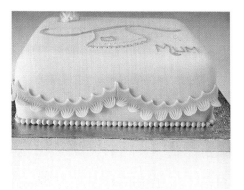

9. Immediately fix the band (with a damp brush) in a curve to half the cake-side (and, if necessary, trim to size). Repeat No's. 7, 8 and 9 to link the bands around the cake.

10. Pipe floral motif dots into each of the band curves. Decorate the cake with artificial flowers and bows.

SELINA

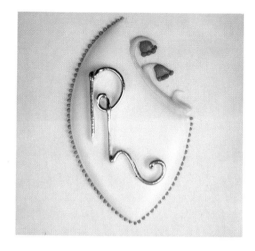

1. Cover a cake with sugarpaste and place it diagonally on a square cake-board. Roll out, cut and fix sugarpaste triangles to the cake-board corners. Then pipe royal icing shells along each cake-base side.

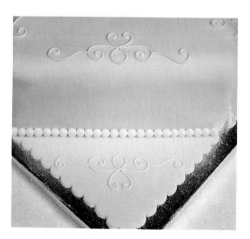

2. Pipe the curved line pattern on the cake-top and board (using the drawing at the bottom of this page as a guide).

3. Overpipe each curved line pattern with bright coloured royal icing.

4. Outline four plaques on waxed paper, using the PLAQUE TEMPLATE as a guide. Flood-in (see Glossary) each plaque and leave to dry for 24 hours. Decorate each plaque with initials of choice.

5. Pipe inscription of choice on cake-top and then decorate cake with artificial flowers and ornaments.

BEFORE COMMENCING THIS CAKE, PLEASE REFER TO THE *IMPORTANT NOTICE* ON PAGE 42.

SELINAS' TEMPLATES

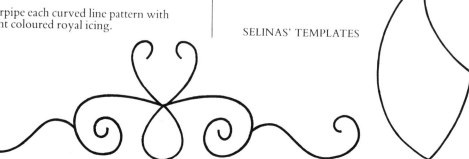

SELINA

NIKKI

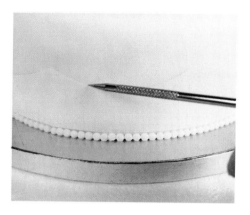

1. Pipe shells around the base of a coated cake. Leave to dry for 30 minutes. Cut a length of paper equal to the circumference of the cake. Fold the paper into eight portions and cut a curve between each portion, as shown. Place band around cake and scribe the curve lines on to the cake side. Remove band.

2. Using cornflour for dusting, roll out a thin sheet of sugarpaste. Then cut a band from it, using an appropriately shaped cutter.

3. Remove surplus sugarpaste and then ensure the band is free from the work surface (and, if necessary, dust work surface with more cornflour).

4. Roll a cocktail stick backwards and forwards over the fluted edge of the band, to create the frill.

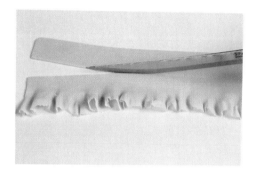

5. Cut the sugarpaste band to the width required.

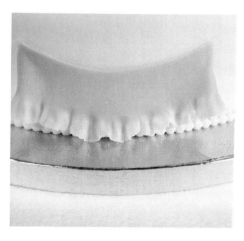

6. Immediately fix the sugarpaste band to one of the scribed curves on the cake-side. (For fixing, brush a thin water line below the scribed line). Trim band to the scribed line length and, using a paint brush, lift out frill base (to give effect shown).

BEFORE COMMENCING THIS CAKE, PLEASE REFER TO THE *IMPORTANT NOTICE* ON PAGE 42.

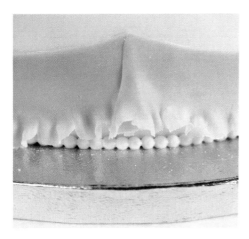

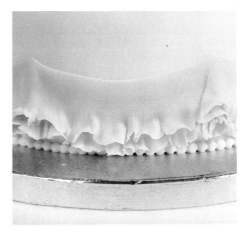

7. Repeat No's. 2-6 for each of the seven remaining scribed lines.

8. Repeat No's. 2-7 over the cake-side frills to form a double frill. Then complete (using the following cake as a guide.

VERINA

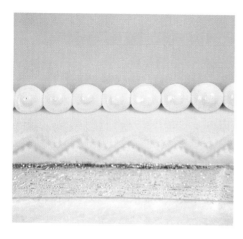

1. Coat each cake and board in sugarpaste. Immediately crimp each cake-board edge. Pipe royal icing bulbs around each cake-base.

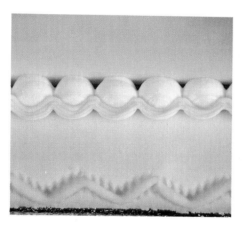

2. Pipe a curved line over each bulb and then overpipe each line *three* times (using a smaller tube each time).

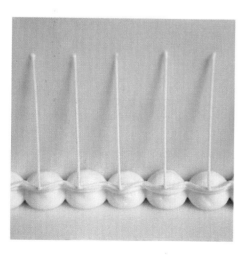

3. Pipe a marker dot on each cake-side (1 inch above each piped bulb). Then pipe a suspended line from each marker dot to the centre of each curved line.

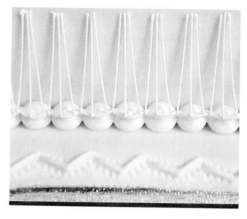

4. Pipe a suspended line each side of the first line, as shown.

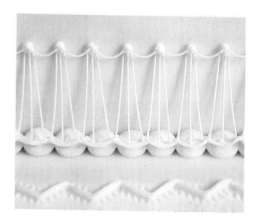

5. Pipe a small bulb over each marker dot and then pipe a suspended curved line between each bulb.

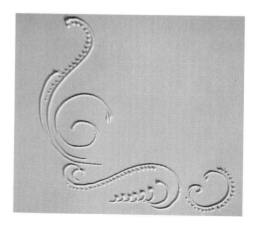

6. Pipe decorative lines and dots on each cake-top corner, as shown. Then pipe a line on each cake-board crimp. Complete the cake with artificial flowers and leaves of choice and cake-board ribbon.

BEFORE COMMENCING THIS CAKE, PLEASE REFER TO THE *IMPORTANT NOTICE* ON PAGE 42.

VERINA

POPPI

POPPI'S TEMPLATE

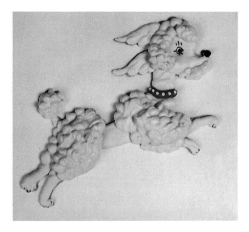

3. Pipe-in the collar and Poppi's nose. Using edible food colouring, brush-in Poppi's eye and paws. Leave to dry for 12 hours.

1. Trace Poppi's template on plain paper and then cover it with waxed paper and fix to a flat surface. Using royal icing (without glycerine) pipe-in the parts shown.

4. Coat an hexagonal cake with sugarpaste and place on a doyley and board. Pipe shells around cake-base.

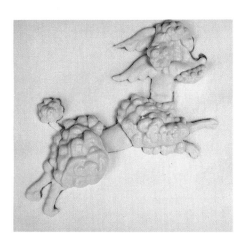

2. Pipe-in the further parts shown (to create Poppi's curly hair). Leave to dry for 12 hours.

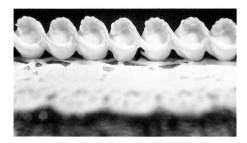

5. Overpipe the shells with 'S' scrolls, as shown. Repeat using a smaller tube.

BEFORE COMMENCING THIS CAKE, PLEASE REFER TO THE *IMPORTANT NOTICE* ON PAGE 42.

6. Decorate each cake-side with piped stems and leaves, artificial flowers and ribbon loops, as shown.

POPPI

7. Decorate cake-top with inscription of choice and piped tracery and dots. Remove Poppi from waxed paper and fix her to the cake-top (jumping through a ribbon hoop).

TRIXIE

1. Roll out and cut a 5″ x 2½″ piece of sugarpaste and immediately crimp the edges. Leave to dry for 24 hours.

2. Pipe message of choice on the plaque, using a fine piping tube.

TRIXIE'S TEMPLATE

3. Place the plaque on the cake-top centre and pipe a series of curved lines around it.

4. Fix flowers of choice over the curved lines, as shown. Pipe leaves to complete the floral decoration.

BEFORE COMMENCING THIS CAKE, PLEASE REFER TO THE *IMPORTANT NOTICE* ON PAGE 42.

TRIXIE

5. Decorate the cake with piped scrolls and shells along the cake-top edges and around the base. Fix narrow ribbon and bows around cake-side in the position shown.

VIOLETTA

Crystallised real flowers are the main decoration of Violetta's cake

1. Thoroughly mix 2 teaspoons of cold water with one fresh egg white. Brush the mixture on the inside petals of a freshly picked violet.

2. Immediately sprinkle fine caster sugar over the damp surface. Carefully shake off the surplus caster sugar.
(NOTE: The whole top surface of the violet should be covered with caster sugar. Repeat the process to cover any bare patches).

3. Upturn the violet and brush the back with the mixture and immediately sprinkle caster sugar over the flower. Gently shake the violet to remove any surplus caster sugar. (Repeat the process to cover any bare patches – as exposure to air will shorten the life of a crystallised flower).

4. Repeat the process to produce some 40 blossoms – leaving them to dry on greaseproof paper on a wire tray and crystallise – about 48 hours in a dry, warm atmosphere.

5. Pipe plain royal icing shells around the cake-base. Leave to dry for 30 minutes, then pipe a line over each shell.

6. Pipe the design shown on each cake-top petal section.

BEFORE COMMENCING THIS CAKE, PLEASE REFER TO THE *IMPORTANT NOTICE* ON PAGE 42.

VIOLETTA

PEPI

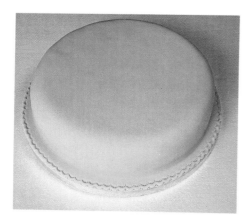

1. Cover a round cake and board with sugarpaste and immediately crimp edge to form a decorative border.

4. Fix discs and petals on cake-top to form flower heads.

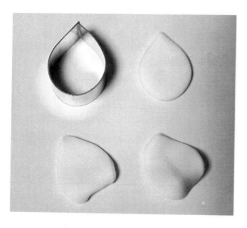

2. Roll out a sheet of sugarpaste and, using a leaf shaped metal cutter, immediately cut three petals. Shape each petal, as shown, then brush confectioners' dusting powder over its centre. (21 petals required).

5. Roll out, cut and fix sugarpaste stems and leaves, as shown.

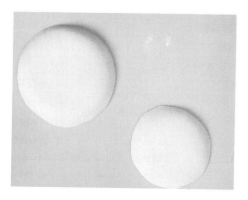

3. Cut and form two domed sugarpaste discs.

6. Decorate flower heads with sugarpaste eyes and piped royal icing features. Add piped inscription of choice.

BEFORE COMMENCING THIS CAKE, PLEASE REFER TO THE *IMPORTANT NOTICE* ON PAGE 42.

PEPI

HARMONY

1. Place a heart-shaped cake on a round cake-board and cover with sugarpaste. Pipe the royal icing scrolls shown around the cake-top edge and base.

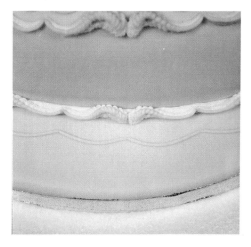

4. Pipe curved lines on the cake-board in the pattern shown.

2. Pipe a line beside each cake-top scroll.

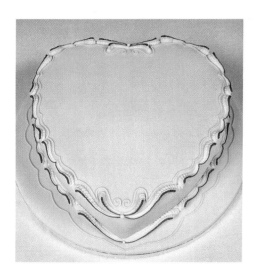

5. Overpipe each scroll with a fine piping tube.

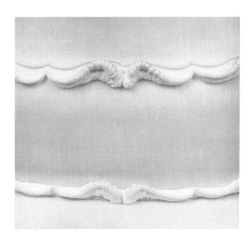

3. Overpipe each cake-top scroll (using a smaller tube).

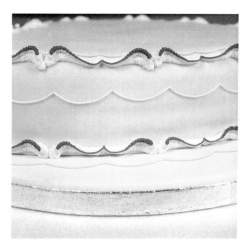

BEFORE COMMENCING THIS CAKE, PLEASE REFER TO THE *IMPORTANT NOTICE* ON PAGE 42.

6. Pipe uniform curved lines around cake side.

7. Make and fix a heart-shaped sugarpaste pillow. Then crimp the pillow edge (see page 22). Decorate cake-top with flowers and piped dots.

8. Make and fix a sugar bell to each alternate cake-side piped curve. Decorate cake-board with flowers, piped dots and edge ribbon. If appropriate, fix artificial rings to pillow.

CHERILYN

CHERILYN'S TEMPLATE

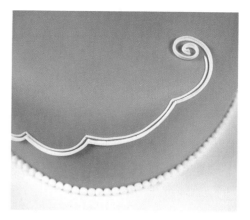

1. Trace each template on greaseproof paper and fix to a tile or other flat surface. Cover with waxed paper and fix in position. using a paper piping bag without a tube – and royal icing without glycerine – pipe the cherubs, as shown. Leave to dry for 24 hours. FOUR CHERUBS REQUIRED FOR EACH CAKE.

3. Pipe a smaller line above each curved line and then overpipe the first lines with the same tube.

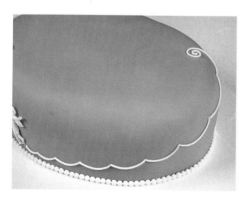

2. Coat each cake with sugarpaste and leave to dry for 24 hours. Coat each board with royal icing. Leave to dry for 12 hours. Pipe plain shells around each cake base. Fix a pair of cherubs to the front and back of each cake. Pipe a series of rising curved lines from each pair of cherubs to end in a whirl on the cake-top.

4. Pipe the floral motif shown in each curve.

BEFORE COMMENCING THIS CAKE, PLEASE REFER TO THE *IMPORTANT NOTICE* ON PAGE 42.

5. Pipe a series of matching curved lines around the cake board, as shown, and then decorate with the floral motifs shown.

CHERILYN

CARINA

1. Place coated sponge cake on a doyley and board. Pipe plain shells around cake base.

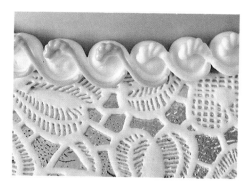

2. Pipe an 'S' scroll over two of the shells and then repeat around the cake (ensuring the 'head' of each scroll overlaps the previous 'tail'). Overpipe each scroll with a smaller tube.

3. Pipe overlapping 'S' scrolls around cake-top edge.

4. Pipe inscription of choice on cake-top and then pipe the tracery and dots shown. Complete the cake with floral and other decorations of choice.

BEFORE COMMENCING THIS CAKE, PLEASE REFER TO THE *IMPORTANT NOTICE* ON PAGE 42.

FENELLA

1. Cover a cake (baked in a 2 pt pudding basin) with sugarpaste and place on a petal shaped cake-board. Then pipe royal icing plain shells around cake-base.

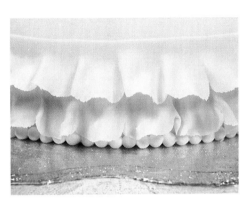

2. Make and fix two layers of sugarpaste frill (see page 76).

3. Make and fix a sugarpaste fluted frill (above the double frill). Fix the crinoline lady's bust to the cake and then surround her waist with sugarpaste petals. Pipe royal icing shells around the waist and on each crinoline frill curve.

4. Decorate each crinoline frill curve with piped royal icing, as shown.

5. Form dress lace by piping royal icing filigree around the cake-top. Then enclose the filigree with a row of piped bows.

BEFORE COMMENCING THIS CAKE, PLEASE REFER TO THE *IMPORTANT NOTICE* ON PAGE 42.

MARY FORD PRODUCTS

The products illustrated represent some of the tools and equipment required to complete the cakes and floral decorations in this book. All are obtainable from the Mary Ford Cake Artistry Centre or local stockist.

LEGEND

1. Floristry ribbon.
2. Edible food colours.
3. Confectioners' dusting powder.
4. Crimpers.
5. Tweezers.
6. Cake smoother.
7. Scriber.
8. Wooden skewers.
9. Piping tubes.
10. Nylon rolling pin.
11. Flower stamens.
12. Floristry wire.
13. Modelling tools.
14. Metal 'flower' cutters.
15. Florists' tape.